York
Travel Guide

*Sightseeing, Hotel, Restaurant
& Shopping Highlights*

Jessica Doherty

Copyright © 2014, Astute Press
All Rights Reserved.

No part of this publication may be reproduced, stored in a retrieval system, or transmitted, in any form or by any means without the prior written permission of the publisher, nor be otherwise circulated in any form of binding or cover other than that in which it is published and without similar condition being imposed on the subsequent purchaser.

If there are any errors or omissions in copyright acknowledgements the publisher will be pleased to insert the appropriate acknowledgement in any subsequent printing of this publication.

Although we have taken all reasonable care in researching this book we make no warranty about the accuracy or completeness of its content and disclaim all liability arising from its use

Table of Contents

York 6
- Culture 9
- Location & Orientation 10
- Climate & When to Visit 13

Sightseeing Highlights 14
- York Minster 14
- Jorvik Viking Centre 16
- National Railway Museum 17
- Clifford's Tower 18
- St. Mary's Abbey 20
- The Shambles (Ancient Street) 21
- Fairfax House 21
- Merchant Adventurer's Hall 23
- City of York Walls 24
- York Castle Museum 25
- York's Chocolate Story 26
- Quilt Museum & Gallery 27
- Holy Trinity Church 28
- Treasurer's House 29
- York Maze 30

Recommendations for the Budget Traveller 32
- Places to Stay 32
  - Hotel Noir 32
  - Alahambra Court Hotel 32
  - Four Seasons Hotel 33
  - The Bloomsbury 33
  - Fort Boutique Hostel 34
- Places to Eat 34
  - Mason's Bar & Bistro 34
  - Bettys 35
  - Krakatoa 35
  - Mumbai Lounge 36
  - Goji Vegetarian Café & Deli 36
- Places to Shop 37
  - Antiques Centre 37

Open Air Market 37
Coppergate Shopping Centre 38
The Cat Gallery 38
Burgins Perfumery 39

York

Located in Northern England, about 200 miles northeast of London, is the medieval, walled city of York. The ancient city is located amidst the green moors and wolds of the North Yorkshire countryside. Encircled by its 13th century walls and its stunning Minster, York still retains its historical charm and heritage. In 2007, York was named the European Tourist City of the Year by European Cities Marketing. New York was named after York when the Duke of York named it in 1664.

The city of York, the ancient capital of Yorkshire, was originally founded by the Romans when they built a fortress in 71 AD. The original name of York was Eboracum. Although there is no official record of the origin of the name, it is believed to be influenced from the Celtic language meaning 'place of the yew trees'. The present name of York, derived from Jorvick (pronounced as Yorwick), was given by the Vikings around 866 AD.

Rarely does one come across a city which has been influenced by so many conquests and communities. Evidence from archeological findings suggest that the earliest settlements in the region was between 8000 – 7000 BC. The Romans found the city in the 1st century AD and ruled for nearly 600 years before the Anglo-Saxon conquest in 627 AD. The Vikings followed with a shorter rule of 2 centuries between 866 – 1066 AD. This was followed by the Normans, the Tudors, the Georgians, and the Victorians in the later centuries, leading right up to the Industrial Revolution in the 19th century.

The city was always a favorite to its rulers. The Roman Emperor Severus made it the capital of Britannia Inferior. After the death of Constantius I, his son, the legendary Constantine the Great was proclaimed emperor in the city fortress. After the Romans abandoned the city, due to the periodic flooding of the Ouse and Foss rivers, the Anglo-Saxon King Edwin claimed the city and made it the chief city of his kingdom. It was under the Anglo-Saxon rule that the city underwent an architectural growth with the building of cathedrals and schools. The Vikings annexed the city in 866 AD and made it an important port for their trade and conquests. Erik Bloodaxe, the last independent Viking ruler of York was the last frontier, whose death brought the unification of England by King Edred.

As a part of unified England, York excelled as a major trading centre in the 12th and the 13th century. Cloth manufacturing reached a peak with York specializing in wool products. Although the city suffered an economic decline in the 16th century under the Tudor rule, it was during this period that the city went through some major religious reforms. Many monastic houses were closed and there was an uprising by the northern Catholics. (Guy Fawkes, the infamous son of York, was found a co-conspirator in the famous Gunpowder Plot of 1605 to displace the Protestant rule.)

It was also during the Tudor rule in 1644 that the city suffered in the Civil War with many houses outside the city wall reduced to ruins. By the late 17th century the cities of Leeds and Hull developed as major centres of trade displacing the monopolistic nature of York. The silting of the River Ouse also affected the river trade. In the 18th and 19th centuries the city grew as an important centre for arts and culture. It saw the construction of many elegant and important buildings like the Theater Royal and the Fairfax House.

The Industrial Revolution provided a boom for York as its importance grew with the establishment of the York and North Midland Railway Company. By the 20th century, thousands were being employed in York by the railway industry. The boom helped establish businesses, the most noteworthy being the chocolate and confectionary business of Rowntree (presently owned by Nestle).

York, with its rich cultural heritage and history has become an attraction to tourists the world over. It is also the home to the York University, one of the foremost universities in the world. The National Railway Museum in York is one of the largest railway museums in the world. The cobbled shopping streets of Stonegate and Petergate still retain the same routes as they did centuries ago. The Shambles (street) in York won the Most Picturesque Street Award in UK in the Google Street View Awards in 2010. (Interesting tip: In York, a 'gate' means a street, and a 'bar' means a gate) Due to the rich treasure cove of archeology and preserved history, the city of York was declared a conservation area in 1968. From the medieval cathedrals to the ghost walks of York 'snickleways', there is entertainment and attractions galore for tourists of every age and interest.

Culture

Culturally, York has a lot to offer with a myriad of festivals and events. After a drink in one of the many famed haunted pubs of York, one can head to catch a performance at the York Theater Royal, which has been producing dramas for over 250 years and is one of the leading producing theaters in the UK. The other popular theater in the city is the Grand Opera House that opened in 1902 and hosts many touring productions.

A must for any theater lover is to catch a performance of the York Mystery Plays (also known as York Corpus Christi Plays). It is a set of 48 pageants (public drama depicting a historical event) covering the Christian history from the Creation to the Last Judgment. These plays date back to the middle of the 14th century. The York Circle of the Mystery Plays is only one of the four existing complete cycle (all 48 plays) of plays. These are usually performed at the York Museum gardens.

The York Early Music Festival held annually every July is dedicated to classical music from the 18th century and earlier. One can also catch a chamber orchestra performance at the St Olave's Church at Marygate. The National Centre for Early Music housed at the 12th century St Mary's Church hosts a number of performances and recordings during the year.

For sports lovers, there is football (soccer), rugby, rowing, and sailing events at York regularly. York has been selected to be a part of the Tour de France 2014. The 18th century award winning York Racecourse holds a number of horse races in summer including the Ebor Race Meeting.

Location & Orientation

Conveniently located in Northern England, York is very well connected by air and land. For those flying in to UK, there are a number of airports to choose from. Although the London airports and the Manchester airport have more flights, one has to travel at least 2 – 2.5 hrs by road or rail to get to York.

The closest airport to York is the Leeds-Bradford International Airport (IATA: LBA). The airport is only 31 miles from York, but the congested Motorways during rush hours can take nearly 1.5 – 2 hrs to commute. Bus number 757 connects the airport to Leeds station; from where one take a direct train connection to York

From any of the London airports (Heathrow – IATA: LHR; Gatwick – IATA: LGW; London City – IATA: LCY; Luton – IATA: LTN; Stansted – IATA: STN), one can take either a rental car or the train and head to York. From Manchester Airport (IATA: MAN), which is 84 miles from York, one can take a train to York. If the journey is scheduled, it is best to buy the train ticket in advance as the tickets are expensive on the day, and one may have to stand for the most part of the 2 hr journey without a reservation.

Other airports in the area are Doncaster-Sheffield (IATA: DSA), Humberside (IATA: HBA), Durham-Tees Valley (IATA: MME), and Newcastle (IATA: NCL).

The York train station was the largest train station in the world when it was built. Voted the nicest train station in the UK in 2007, it is very well connected with all the major cities in the country. The fastest trains can take one to London in less than 2 hrs. Other cities connected from York include Manchester (1 hr 24 min), Nottingham (2 hrs), Sheffield (1 hr), Newcastle (1 hr), Bristol (4 hrs), and Liverpool (2 hrs).

There are a number of rail operators including East Coast (Tel: 08457 225 111; http://www.eastcoast.co.uk/), Grand Central (Tel: 0844 811 0071; http://www.grandcentralrail.com/), Transpennine (Tel: 0844 556 5637; http://www.tpexpress.co.uk/), Northern Rail (Tel: 0844 241 3454; http://www.northernrail.org/), and Cross Country (Tel: 08447 369 123; http://www.crosscountrytrains.co.uk/). These websites often have online discounts for buying tickets in advance.

National Express - http://www.nationalexpress.com - runs buses throughout UK and connects York with a number of cities. An average journey time between London and York is between 5 – 6 hrs and costs approximately £30 one way.

For those driving in to the city by car, York is 20 min from the M1/M62 motorway network. York has the facility of 'Park and Ride' - http://www.itravelyork.info/park-and-ride, one can park the car for free outside the city at a designated parking space and ride a bus in to the city.

Once a famed port city, York is connected by ferry service - http://www.poferries.com/ - too. The terminal for York is Kingston-upon-Hull. The port is connected to the city by bus service.

Within the city, one can see the old city and the major attractions by foot. Many of the tourist places have been made auto free zones making it a very comfortable walk. Even if one has a car, it is best to park it in a Park and Ride spot and take any of the color-coded busses to the various tourist spots. A onetime trip, in any of these buses, costs £2, and is free for children.

There is a bus service within the city and but it can be expensive if one is planning multiple trips (a single adult ticket costs £3.50). It is best to buy the All York Day single bus pass for £5. The All York Family bus pass costs £10, and allows a family of 5 with maximum 2 adults. Taxis can be cheaper for a group of 3 - 4 people. Taxi companies in York include Streamline Taxis (Tel: 01904 656565) and York Cars (Tel: 01904 765765).

Another option to move in the narrow lanes of York is bicycles. York is very cycle friendly with a bicycle friendly traffic system. There are a number of cycle paths and bicycle parking spots across the city. It is important to follow the rules while cycling in York as a penalty could be very steep. The York Cycle Map - http://www.york.gov.uk/cycling/ - has details of the cycling paths and parking spots.

Climate & When to Visit

York is located in the temperate climate zone that results in mild summers and near-freezing winters. As it is located in the vast and open Vale of York, it is often hit by cold freezing winds and frost. The summer temperature stays in the mid 20s and rarely touches a high of 30 degrees Celsius. Winter temperatures go to near freezing and there may be light snow from Dec to April. There is precipitation all the year round with the wettest months from Nov - Jan.

York is best visited during spring and summertime between the months of April – Sep. The mild weather (highs of around 25 degrees Celsius and lows of about 12 degrees Celsius) and limited precipitation makes it an ideal time for tourism.

Sightseeing Highlights

Tourists visiting York should opt for the York Pass – http://www.yorkpass.com/ . The Pass allows cash free entry to 30 attractions in York, and discounts at a number of stores. The 2 day pass costs £43.20 and the 3 day pass costs £52.20. It also includes a guidebook.

York Minster

Church House, Ogleforth, York
Tel: 0844 939 0011
http://www.yorkminster.org/

Dominating the York skyline is the majestic York Minster, one of the largest cathedrals in Northern Europe.

It is presently the seat of the Archbishop of York, the 2nd highest office of the Church of England. The Minster (cathedral) has a length of 520 ft and has an imposing 200 ft central tower and 174 ft western towers.

First record of the church dates back to 627 AD when the structure was made of wood. It was replaced by a stone building in 637 AD. Over the next few centuries, the church went through numerous disrepair, destruction, restoration, and expansion. One of the major expansions was in 741 AD when 30 altars were built. The Normans restored and expanded it in their signature style in 1080 and remodeled the choir and the crypt a century later.

The imposing Gothic style remodeling and building started in the 13th century and went on till the 15th century when it was consecrated in 1472. In the 18th century, the floor was re-laid with marble. Restoration continued even in the 2nd half of the 20th century to strengthen the central tower which was close to collapsing.

The cathedral has beautiful stained glass windows – the 16 m high Five Sisters lancet windows in the north; the Rose Window in the south, and the famed Heart Window in the west. There is extensive use of stained glass throughout the church with some dating back to the 12th century. The roof of the Chapter House is made of wood with a beautiful innovative design. The present organ in the church was built in 1832; it is still in use but had gone through a number of repairs due to wear and tear, and a fire in 1984.

The Minster Library has a large collection of historic printed books and documents. There are over 250000 artifacts from the pre medieval period. One can have access to these artifacts by prior appointment on Monday, Tuesday, and Wednesday. The Undercroft of the Minster is being remodeled to have a state of the art audio visual experience for the visitors. Work is scheduled to finish by 2016. The Minster also organizes a number of musical events, conferences, and activities throughout the year.

There are a variety of ticket combinations and prices. Ticket prices for Minster and the Tower are: Adult – £14; child – £3.50. One can also buy a Family Pass depending on the number of adults and children in the group. The Minster ticket includes a free guided tour.

The Minster is open Mon – Sat from 9:00 am – 5:30 pm, and on Sunday from 12 noon to 3:45 pm. It is closed on Good Friday and Easter Saturday.

Jorvik Viking Centre

Coppergate, York
Tel: 01904 615505
http://www.jorvik-viking-centre.co.uk/

The Jorvik Viking Centre is a museum built on the very site where archeological excavations unearthed 250000 pieces of pottery, 40000 artifacts, and nearly 5 tons of animal bone from the Viking era.

A monorail takes the visitor through a number of exhibits recreated as in the Viking era. The recreation does not only limit itself to the layout of the houses (as in a Viking village) or the chattering of the neighbors, but also recreates the smell and the stench of the kitchen and the cesspit. Interesting displays include the copper helmet, the silk hat, the sword pommel, along with weapons and jewelry from the Viking age. The Viking Centre also organizes a number of activities and festivals related to the Vikings including the 'Dig' where one gets to do hands-on excavating.

A ticket of the Jorvik Viking Centre entitles the user unlimited entry for one year. There are a number of combo tickets available for entry to the Viking Centre, the Dig, the Barley Hall, and the Micklegate Bar. An adult ticket only for the Viking Centre costs £9.75 (for a child £6.75). Family tickets are also available. With a £1 premium online ticket, one can skip the queue and choose a time slot of one's visit.

The Centre is open every day from 10:00 am – 5:00 am. The closing time, however changes during festivals (at 6:00 pm) and winter months (at 4:00 pm).

National Railway Museum

Leeman Road, York
Tel: 08448 153139
http://www.nrm.org.uk/

With over 300 years of history and over a million objects related to the railways, the award winning National Railway Museum is the largest railway museum in the world.

There are over 100 locomotives in display including some historical ones like the Rocket – the first modern steam engine, the Duchess of Hamilton, the Shinkansen bullet train, and the famous Flying Scotsman. It also has on display some of the royal trains used by Queen Victoria and Edward VII. The museum also has a live railway workshop. There is a miniature railway ride for children. The displayed trains and the model stations can make one travel back in time with the intricately detailed work.

The Mallard Experience – dedicated to the world's fastest steam locomotive of its time – is a special simulated ride of the locomotive. Some of the original members of the ride are also present at the Hall. The museum has storytelling sessions for children of 3 – 7 years.

The main Museum is open on all days from 10:00 am – 6:00 pm and has free entry. The Mallard Experience tickets cost: Adult – £5; Child – £4. Although there is free entry to the museum, a voluntary donation of £3 is collected from visitors.

Clifford's Tower

Tower Street, York
Tel: 01904 646940
http://www.english-heritage.org.uk/daysout/properties/cliffords-tower-york/

The now-ruinous Clifford's Tower is the keep to the York Castle that was built by the Normans in 1068.

The quatrefoil design with 4 overlapping circles like a four-leafed clover, with a curtain wall and gatehouse, is reminiscent of the Chateau d'Etampes near Paris.

The original tower built by William the Conqueror was made of wood and was burnt down a century later after the infamous Jewish Massacre at the site. A restored wooden tower of 1194 was again destroyed by gale in 1245. Henry III commissioned the re-building of the tower in stone. Engineers were brought from the Windsor Castle, and the present quatrefoil tower standing 15 m high was built. The tower was mostly used as a military base and a prison camp for the next few centuries. There were also a number of political executions at the location. The tower, originally called the King's Tower, is rumored to have its present moniker after Roger de Clifford was executed there for opposing Edward II.

The tower stands on a hill with a remodeled stone approach. There is a circular stairway that takes one to the top of the tower. On a clear day, one can have an excellent panoramic view of the city of York.

The Tower is owned and maintained by the English Heritage and there is free entry for its members. For others the ticket prices are: Adult – £4.20; Child – £2.50; Family Ticket (2 adults and 3 children) – £10.90

The tower is open from 10:00 am – 6:00 pm with reduced hours from Nov – Mar (closing at 4:00pm). It is closed on 24, 25, and 26 Dec, and on Jan 1st.

St. Mary's Abbey

Marygate
York

Set against the gardens of the Yorkshire Museum, the ruins of St. Abbey is a mere shadow of what was once the most powerful and wealthiest monastery of Northern England. The foundation of this Benedictine monastery was laid by William II in the 11th century.

The abbey's walls were extended in the 12th century making it over three quarters of a mile long. In the early 14th century, royal permission was given to raise the walls with crenels. A part of this wall still exists along Marygate to the River Ouse. During the dissolution and destruction of the monasteries after the decree from Henry VIII in 1539, St Mary's was the richest and largest Benedictine monastery in Northern England.

One can still see the main entrance, now the ruined Gatehouse, run from the river to the monastery. Although the abbey was destroyed, the 15th century Abbot's House (renamed as King's Manor) survived as it was used as a seat of the Council. One can also see remains of the wooden 14th century Pilgrims' Hospitium – the hospitality and lodging centre for the pilgrims. The museum gardens and the Hospitium garden are popular wedding and picnic spots.

The St. Mary's Abbey is right across the Yorkshire Museum and close to the Minster, and has free entry.

The Shambles (Ancient Street)

http://www.insideyork.co.uk/what-to-see/shambles.html

The narrow cobbled street is claimed to be Europe's most visited street. Winner of the Britain's Most Picturesque Street Award in 2010, Shambles has retained the charm and flavor of a busy medieval shopping street. The name originates from shamel which means boot or shelf. The street was also called Flesshammel meaning 'shelves of meat' as the street supposedly had 26 butcher shops in the late 19th century and the meat was displayed or served at the shop window shelves. The street does not have any of the butcher shops but one can still see the meat-hanging hooks outside some of the stores. Shambles is lined on both sides with 15th century Tudor buildings that overhang the street by several feet giving a feel that those would almost fall on the head of a passer-by!

The Shambles is dotted with souvenir shops and eateries. One can take a ghost walk or a historic walk along Shambles. The oldest street in York and one of the best preserved medieval streets in the world.

Fairfax House

Castlegate, York
Tel: 01904 655 543
http://www.fairfaxhouse.co.uk

This Georgian architectural marvel was designed by the 18th century architect John Carr.

The Fairfax House was built in 1762 by Count Viscount Fairfax as a winter retreat for his family. It was intended to be a dowry for his only surviving child – Anne, but as Anne never got married, Viscount Fairfax got the 3 storied house redesigned by Carr. Intricate artwork, expensive mahogany furniture, and decorative ceilings and reliefs made it one of the finest private houses of Northern England.

The House changed ownership a number of times and was used by the military in World War I. By the end of the war, the House was home to the 1000-seater St George's Cinema and Dancehall. With slumping business and disrepair, the York Civic Trust stepped in in 1982 to restore the building to its former glory.

The Fairfax House today has 2 floors of one of the finest private collections of Georgian furniture, paintings, and decorative art. There are guided tours, exhibitions, and special events. The Fairfax House celebrates 250 years in 2013.

Ticket prices for entry to the House: Adult - £6 (allows unlimited entry for 1 year). Children under 16 and accompanied by an adult enter free. There are guided tours on Mondays between 11:00 am and 2:00 pm.

The seasonal opening of the Fairfax House is from Feb – Dec. Exact dates may be checked at the website. It is open Tues to Sat from 10:00 am – 5:00 pm and on Sunday from 12:30 pm – 4:00 pm. It is closed from Dec 24 – 26, and from Jan till early Feb.

Merchant Adventurer's Hall

Fossgate, York
Tel: 01904 654818
http://www.theyorkcompany.co.uk/

This marvelous medieval wooden building was built by a religious fraternity (called Guild of Our Lord Jesus and The Blessed Virgin Mary) of York right at the city centre as a place for meetings, worship, and business. The building was built between 1357 and 1361 and is a Grade I listed building (which means it has the highest listing on the Statutory List of Buildings of Special Architectural or Historic Interest in the UK alongside buildings like the Royal Albert Hall and the Palace of Westminster).

The Hall has 3 main rooms – the Great Hall for conducting business, the Undercroft as an alms house for the poor, and the Chapel as a place of worship. The timber framed Great Hall took 5 years to complete and is the largest wooden framed structure in the UK which is still in use for its original purpose. The Chapel is also still used as a place for worship. The Hall is used as an everyday base for the Company of Merchant Adventurers of the City of York.

The Hall houses a beautiful collection of oil paintings, silver artifacts, and furniture. Some of the portraits on the walls are of former Governors of the Company. One of the oldest pieces in the collection is a 14th century oak evidence chest. The surrounding of the Hall was developed into a garden and was used as a rest area after the First World War. The Hall is fully accessible to the public through the Fossgate entrance.

The Hall is given out on private hires for weddings, corporate meetings, and dinners.

Ticket prices to enter the Merchant Adventurer's Hall: Adult – £6 (free entry for children under 16).

The Hall is open all days from Mar – Oct from 9:00 am – 5:00 pm (reduced hours on weekends); and from Nov – Feb from 9:00 am – 4:00 pm (reduced hours on Fri & Sat; Sundays closed). It is closed from Dec 24 – Jan 01. Please note that the Hall is closed occasionally for functions and private events.

City of York Walls

York

The protective walls around the city of York were built during the Roman era. Over centuries the Walls have been expanded and restructured to serve its purpose. The surviving 4.5 miles of Walls are the most complete example of existing medieval walls in the UK. The Multangular Tower is the only intact part of the Wall from the Roman era. Most of the existing Walls are from the Norman rule from the 12th – 14th century when the palisades were replaced by crenellated stone walls. The bar Walls had 6 bars or gatehouses (gateways).

These gatehouses acted as checkpoints for traffic moving in and out of the perimeters of the City Walls. These were also the points where toll was collected. 4 out of the 6 were major bars, namely, the Bootham Bar, the Monk Bar, the Walmgate Bar, and the Micklegate Bar. The Bootham bar is the oldest with some stonework dating back to the 11th century. The 4 storey Monk Bar is the tallest and most elaborate and houses the Richard III Museum. The Walmgate Bar is the only existing bar in England with a barbican (a fortified outer gate). The Micklegate Bar which leads to the Viking ruins of York was the traditional ceremonial entry gate for monarchs. The 2 minor bars are Fishergate Bar (near George Street) and Victoria Bar (was abandoned and blocked after a few years).

The City Walls provide an excellent panoramic view of the city. Although a complete walk on the Walls takes about 2 hours, the best views are between the Bootham Bar and the Monk Bar, a short 15 minute stretch encircling the Minster. It's a free walk and is best enjoyed on a clear sunny day.

York Castle Museum

The Eye of York
Tel: 01904 687687
http://www.yorkcastlemuseum.org.uk/

The York Castle Museum was founded in 1938 by Dr John Kirk, and is housed in the prison buildings of the 11th century York Castle built by William the Conqueror. The highlight of the museum is the Kirkgate - a recreated Victorian street named after the founder, Dr Kirk.

The iconic recreation features cobbled streets, police cell, schoolroom, and original businesses from that period. It even has actors playing characters from the Victorian era. The other galleries include the Toy Gallery, The York Castle Prison, and The Raindale Mill.

Tickets to the Castle Museum cost: Adult – £8.50 (free for children under 16). A ticket is valid for unlimited entry for one year. It is wheelchair accessible and 1 carrier is allowed free entry with the visitor.

The Museum is open daily from 9:30 am – 5:00 pm (with a 2:30 pm closure on Dec 24 and 31). It is closed on Dec 25 & 26, and Jan 1.

York's Chocolate Story

Kings Square
York
Tel: 0845 498 9411
http://yorkschocolatestory.com/

Located in Kings Square in the heart of York, the York's Chocolate Story is a guided tour through the history of chocolate and the "chocolate families" of York. York has contributed to the world of chocolates through the famous Kit Kat, Polo, and Chocolate Orange.

The Story has a number of Zones including the Story Zone – discovery of cocoa beans to its travel to York centuries later; Factory Zone – displaying how the beans are made into chocolate and the founding of York's famous chocolate companies; and Indulgence Zone – the chocolate tasting café. York is the home of chocolates in the UK, still producing over a billion Kit Kats every year. The York's Chocolate Story pays tribute to this historical journey of chocolate in York.

Ticket prices are: Adult – £8.50; Child – £7.50. There is a 15% discount if tickets are bought online.

It is open daily from 10:00 am – 6:30 pm with extended hours in summer. It is closed on Dec 25 and Jan 1.

Quilt Museum & Gallery

St Anthony's Hall, Peasholme Green
York
Tel: 01904 613242
http://www.quiltmuseum.org.uk/

Opened in 2008, the Quilt Museum and Gallery is the first museum in Britain dedicated to quilt making and textile arts. It is housed at the St Anthony's Hall, one of the only 4 remaining guild halls in the city of York. The gallery has a unique collection of quilts and silk work dating back to the 18th century.

Ticket prices are: Adult – £6. Free entry for children.

It is open Mon – Sat from 10:00 am – 4:00 pm and closed on Sunday. The Gallery is closed during winter and exhibition changeover weeks. Details of the dates are posted in the website.

Holy Trinity Church

70 Goodramgate
York
http://www.visitchurches.org.uk/Ourchurches/Completelistofchurches/Holy-Trinity-Church-York-North-Yorkshire/

Located in a garden behind Goodramgate, one of York's busiest shopping streets, the 12th century Holy Trinity Church is a hidden wonder of the city.

Although the foundation was laid in the 12th century, the church building that we see today was completed around the 15th century. The Minster Tower and the church are devoid of any grandeur but are beautiful in their simplicity. Noteworthy are the 17th century pew boxes and 15th century stained glass windows that have survived through time. The Church is one of the many maintained by The Churches Conservation Trust.

The Church has free entry but one can give donations.

The Church is open Tues – Sat from 10:00 am – 4:00pm, and Sun – Mon from 12 noon – 4:00 pm.

Treasurer's House

Minster Yard
York
Tel: 01904 624247
http://www.nationaltrust.org.uk/treasurers-house-york/

Owned and maintained by the National Trust, the centuries old Treasurer's House is a stone's throw from the York Minster. It is one of the popular haunted houses in the city and was featured in the TV series Ghostbusters.

The House used to be the home to the treasurer of the York Minster. Although it has gone through many ownerships and restorations over the centuries, it carries with it a history of nearly 2000 years through a road in the cellar which is believed to have been laid during the Roman era. The House has a beautiful collection of artifacts displayed through the Attic Tour and the Cellar Tour. Every spring the House opens its '2000 white tulip' garden to the public.

Ticket prices to enter the property: Adult – £5.90; Child – £2.95. Cellar and Attic Tours charges apply.

It is open Sat – Thurs from 11:00 am – 4:30 pm. Friday closed. It is closed in the winter months. Season dates are posted in the website.

York Maze

Tel: 01904607341
http://www.yorkmaze.com/

Located less than 2.5 miles from the York Station, the York Maze is the largest maze in Britain and one of the largest in the world. Perfect for a day out with kids, the maze has a lot of activities to keep the young and the young-at-heart entertained. The huge maze is made from more than 1 million maize plants. Some of the other attractions in the Maze include The Water Ways, Quads Bikes, The Climbing Zone, Pig Racing, the Inflatable Slide, and Remote Control Boats.

There are restaurants and cafes for refreshments. As the Maze is out on the country side, one should check the local bus timings so as not to miss the last returning bus from the Maze. The bus ticket should be retained as it gets a £1 discount for every ticket.

The Maze is usually open daily between July and Sep every year from 10:00 am – 6:30 pm. Season dates are posted on the website.

Ticket prices are: Adult – £11.50; Child – £10.50. Family tickets and online discounts are available.

Some other attractions in York are: The Guildhall, Yorkshire Lavender Gardens, St Michael le Belfrey Church, The Wheel of York, York Cold War Bunker, Roman Bath Public House, Madhyamaka Buddhist Centre, Captain Cook Memorial Museum, Byland Abbey, and the Eden Park.

Recommendations for the Budget Traveller

Places to Stay

Hotel Noir

3 – 5 Clifton Green, York
Tel: 0800 612 8008
http://www.hotelnoir.co.uk/

The hotel is a 10 min walk from the Minster. There are a variety of rooms ranging from Compact to Family Rooms. All 28 rooms have basic amenities including a hot drinks machine, a mini bar, and complimentary toiletries. Room rates vary from day to day and start from £50 per person. There are discounts for advance online bookings.

Alahambra Court Hotel

31 St. Mary's, Bootham, York
Tel: 01904 617427
http://www.alhambracourthotel.co.uk/

The hotel is in a Georgian townhouse and located just a few hundred meters from the York Minster.

It has a candle lit bar and a restaurant serving English and continental dishes. All the 24 rooms are suite styled with all basic amenities. Room rates start from £35 per person per night (pppn) and include English breakfast.

Four Seasons Hotel

7 St Peter's Grove, Bootham
York
Tel: 01904 622621
http://www.fourseasons-hotel.co.uk/

Located in a quiet street less than a mile from the Minster, this home based non-smoking hotel has only 4 rooms so it is a good idea to book well in advance. Each beautifully decorated room is named after a season – spring, summer, autumn, and winter. The Hotel does not take single night bookings and charges 2.5% on credit card transactions. Tariff starts from £49 pppn.

The Bloomsbury

127 Clifton
York
Tel: 01904 634031

This tastefully decorated B&B hotel is a 20 minute walk from the city centre. With spacious rooms and excellent service, the hotel has become quite popular after it changed ownership in 2009.

One should check the website for driving directions to the hotel as those provide a more picturesque and traffic-free ride as compared to the ones in the Internet. Room rates start from £45 and include breakfast.

Fort Boutique Hostel

1 Stonegate
York
Tel: 01904 639573
http://www.thefortyork.co.uk/

This is York's first boutique hostel and was voted one of the top 10 hostels by 'HostelWorld' and 'UK – Visit Britain'. It is located close to the city centre and has designer rooms and décor. The Hostel has a bar-cum-restaurant where one can also catch a live musical performance. Tariff starts from £18 pppn for the 8 bed mixed dorm to £38 pppn for the twin rooms.

Places to Eat

Mason's Bar & Bistro

13 Fossgate, York
Tel: 01904 611919
http://www.masonsbarbistro.co.uk

The eatery serves primarily British cuisine along with some popular fast food. Starters start from £3 and the main course and skewers are priced about £11 making it a very pocket friendly restaurant.

There is a special menu served during Christmas. The eatery was once the home of a high quality grocer; some of the original features have been retained to give a warm homely character. It is open from 12 noon – 9:30 pm daily with an afternoon break from 3:00pm – 5:30pm from Mon – Fri.

Bettys

Harrowgate, Stonegate, York
Tel: 0845 600 1919
http://www.bettys.co.uk/

Established near a century ago, in the year of its phone number 1919, Bettys is a favorite for cakes, tea, and almost anything English.

There are 6 Bettys café outlets in York. The house specialty is the Fat Rascal – a huge buttery fruit scone. Bettys has become a brand over the years and sells branded food items and products. It is open 8:30 am – 5:30 pm from Mon – Fri excluding bank holidays.

Krakatoa

39 Tanner Row, York
Tel: 01904 633066

It is a good idea to reserve a table before heading to the Krakatoa as this Indonesian restaurant is usually chock-a-block.

The restaurant is a 55-seater with a unique hand painted interior décor. It has built a reputation in York with its spicy Indonesian cuisine and excellent service. During lunch hours, along with ala carte, the restaurant serves a set 2-course box lunch for £9.50.

Mumbai Lounge

47 Fossgate, York
Tel: 01904 654155
http://www.mumbailoungeyork.co.uk/

North Indian cuisine is very popular in the UK, and Mumbai Lounge keeps the flag flying in York. The restaurant also serves Bangladeshi cuisine.

One can have a 4-course combo lunch here for less than £7. There is a lounge upstairs where one can bring one's own music to listen to. It is open from 12 noon till midnight daily. It is closed for Friday lunch.

Goji Vegetarian Café & Deli

38 Goodramgate, York
Tel: 01904 622614
http://www.gojicafe.co.uk/

This café cum take-away joint serves vegetarian and vegan food. They also have special items for gluten-intolerant and nut-intolerant guests.

Widely recommended is the mushroom burger. A must visit for even the non-vegetarians. The deli is open from 11:00am – 4:30 pm (opens at 9:30am on Fri & Sat). The restaurant is open on Fri & Sat from 6:30 pm – 11:00 pm.

Places to Shop

Antiques Centre

41 Stonegate, York
Tel: 01904 635888
http://www.theantiquescentreyork.co.uk/

The store houses 5 showrooms in 3 floors in a Georgian townhouse.

There are over a 100 dealers with antique items and collectibles ranging from a Stone Age Chopping Tool to an ancient Greek Terracotta Oil Lamp. Even browsing through the huge collections in the stores can take a couple of hours. The store also sells items online.

Open Air Market

Newgate

The Market is in the city centre close to the Shambles. It has over a 100 stalls selling a variety of products ranging from fresh produce to local clothes and crafts. The market is a good place to get local products at a good bargain. It is open daily except Jan1, Dec 25 & 26.

Coppergate Shopping Centre

12 Coppergate Walk
York
Tel: 01904 627 160
http://www.coppergateshoppingcentre.co.uk/

This shopping centre is within the York city walls and houses the Jorvik Viking Centre. There are a wide variety of stores and eateries including brands like Ark, The Body Shop, The Whisky Shop, and Starbucks. It is open Mon – Thurs from 9:00 am – 5:30 pm, Fri & Sat from 9:00 am – 6:00 pm, and sun from 10:30 am – 5:00 pm.

The Cat Gallery

45 Low Petergate
York
Tel: 01904 631611
http://www.thecatgallery.co.uk/

One of the popular trails in York is the Cat Trail leading through some of York's most popular attractions. There are a number of stores that sell 'cat products' with The Cat Gallery standing out for its variety and pocket friendly pricing. There is jewelry to home wares with cat designs. It is a great place to buy small gifts. The store is open Mon – Sat from 10:00 am – 5:00 pm, and from 11:00 am on Sundays.

Burgins Perfumery

2 Coney Street
York
Tel: 01904 623137
http://www.burginsofyork.co.uk/

Established in 1880 as a chemist and a perfumery store, Burgins Perfumery is now a dedicated perfumery since 1972. Located in a beautifully decorated corner store it sells a very wide variety of perfumes including the major global brands. The store also sells bath products and grooming products for men.

Other shopping sites: Shambles is one of the most popular streets for shopping in York. Details and links are given in the 'Sightseeing Highlights' Section.

Printed in Great Britain
by Amazon